D0277720

Black Bart, the Welsh Pirate

First published: May 2005

© text: Myrddin ap Dafydd 2005
© illustrations: James Field 2005
© English text: Siân Lewis 2005

ISBN: 0 86381-985-0

Cover design: Design Department of the Welsh Books Council

Published with the financial support of the
Welsh Books Council

Printed in Italy

Published by
Gwasg Carreg Gwalch, 12 Iard yr Orsaf, Llanrwst, Wales LL26 0EH
℡ 01492 642031 📠 01492 641502
📧 books@carreg-gwalch.co.uk
Internet: www.carreg-gwalch.co.uk

Black Bart, the Welsh Pirate

Myrddin ap Dafydd
Translated by Siân Lewis
Illustrated by James Field

Nowhere in Wales is far from the sea. It is no wonder then that the sea has played an important part in the country's history. There are smooth yellow beaches on the coast – but there are also sheer cliffs and jagged rocks.

In the old days the people living on the coast were as varied as the landscape itself. Some were sailors and fishermen who lived quiet and peaceful lives, but others were ruthless men who lived dangerously. Many people were smugglers and they used to hide goods such as brandy and tobacco in caves along the Welsh coast. In other places wreckers lit fires to lure unsuspecting ships onto the rocks, and then they stole their cargoes.

But Wales is most famous for its pirates. These pirates were daring sailors who could also be very cruel. For them life was a great adventure. The most successful pirate ever was a man from Pembrokeshire who was called Bartholomew Roberts, but who was known as Black Bart.

Black Bart was born just over three hundred years ago in the quiet village of Little Newcastle in the depths of the Pembrokeshire countryside. When he was a boy, Bart's life was connected with the land rather than the sea. His cheeky smile and his mop of curly black hair made him a great favourite with everyone in the village where he lived – everyone, that is, except the local gamekeeper.

Bart's father was a poor clog maker and the family often went short of food. To help out, Bart caught rabbits and poached fish from the river on the squire's land. It was the gamekeeper's job to protect the animals on the land and in the river, so of course he was after Bart's blood! But Bart was far too clever to be caught.

Bart enjoyed making fun of the poor gamekeeper. Once he put a piece of turf on the top of the keeper's chimney, which made all the smoke blow back into the cottage. The mischievous boy hid behind the hedge and choked with laughter when the keeper ran out of his house red-eyed and coughing.

When the squire got to hear of Bart's tricks, he was furious, and he made life very difficult for the boy. At that time in Wales it was dangerous for

someone to anger the squire, so when Bart was thirteen – like many other young lads – he decided to go to sea.

At first Bart worked on the big sailing ships that carried goods across the oceans. He sailed to the West Indies to pick up a load of sugar. He sailed to Africa and returned with a cargo of slaves. He sailed to India and the Far East to fetch a load of dishes and rich spices.

From the very beginning Bart loved the seafaring life. The sound of the wind in the sails and the lapping of the waves against the hull was music to him. Even when storms blew up on the roughest seas, Bart merely laughed and revelled in the drama and excitement of it all. Love of the sea had entered the blood of the Pembrokeshire boy.

Bart worked on many different ships and it didn't take long for the captains to realise that he was a natural sailor. Many gave him responsible positions, and after twenty years at sea he had been made Second Mate. He was on a ship that was sailing back to Bristol from the Far East when the whole course of his life changed.

His ship was sailing across a bay off the French coast. The wind was light and the sea was

calm. Black Bart was relaxing on deck when he saw another ship heading towards them.

It was a strange-looking ship. As it drew near, Bart saw with dismay that it was painted black all over. It was a pirate ship! He shouted to his sailors and called for his captain, but it was too late to escape. The pirate ship was much faster than Bart's ship which was slowed down by its heavy load. The pirates quickly drew up alongside, launched their grappling hooks and scrambled along the ropes towards them. Bart looked at the hard, scarred faces of the pirates.

He drew his sword. "Arm yourselves! Grab cudgels and whips," he yelled at his crew. "We must drive them off."

But a crew of ordinary sailors stood no chance against the determined and experienced pirates. In no time the gang from the black ship had overpowered Bart's crew and taken them prisoner.

"What will happen now?" Black Bart wondered. He had often been told how cruel and vicious pirates could be.

While he was standing on deck awaiting his doom, Bart began to listen closely. He heard a very familiar sound. After so many years at sea, Black

Bart was used to hearing many foreign languages, but this was different: the language he heard was his own – the pirates were speaking Welsh to each other!

"Well, this is a fine kettle of fish," he said out loud in Welsh.

"What did you say?" asked an astonished pirate. "Hey, Elsyn. This one's a Welshman! Go and tell the captain."

Soon the pirate captain – a man from Carmarthen named Hywel Dafydd – was chatting with the sailor from Little Newcastle.

"It's a small world," he marvelled. "Listen, Bart, once we've helped ourselves to your cargo, we'll be sailing for the coasts of Spain and Africa. I've seen how well you can fight. How about joining us for a bit of an adventure?"

Bart jumped at the chance. Soon he stepped aboard the black ship and the course of his life changed once again.

From the very first he impressed the pirates. He was
even more daring than the bravest of their crew. In
no time Captain Hywel Dafydd had made him
First Mate. Bart was a natural leader: he treated
the crew fairly but made sure they kept to the rules.

Bart began to enjoy the daily excitement and
the riches that were now part of his life.

Then disaster struck. As the pirates were
attacking and boarding a ship off the African coast,
Captain Hywel Dafydd was shot dead. Black Bart
had only been a pirate for six short weeks. What
would happen now? After they had overrun the
ship, stolen its treasure and sailed far enough off,
the pirate crew gathered on deck to hold a meeting
and choose a new captain. Who would the new
captain be?

There was only one name on everyone's lips:
"Black Bart!

"Black Bart from Little Newcastle!"

The crew were pleased with their new captain. Bart believed in keeping good order onboard ship. The pirates under his command were not allowed to gamble, swear, quarrel or fight amongst themselves and they had to put their lights out by eight o'clock every night. Nor were they allowed to take strong drink while at sea. Throughout his life Bart never touched a drop of wine or brandy – his favourite drink was a cup of tea!

Sunday was a special day for Bart. He would never assault another ship on a Sunday and he often held religious services on deck. It's hard to imagine a crowed of pirates singing hymns at the top of their voice – but that's how it was on Bart's ship!

Whenever a new man joined the pirate crew, he had to place his hand on a Welsh Bible and swear an oath of allegiance to the captain.

In spite of his strictness, the pirates thought the world of Bart. When any of them were injured in battle, Bart would pay for them to have treatment on shore. Old pirates who retired were even given a pension – Bart was a man before his time!

More than anything, however, the pirates admired Black Bart for his courage and his success. He was afraid of nothing and no one and as he usually managed to win his battles, he made his crew very rich.

In those days ships from Spain, Portugal and England used to sail to Central and South America and steal vast amounts of gold and treasure from the people who lived there. All that the pirates had to do was to capture these ships as they made their way back to Europe, and lighten their load. After all, to their way of thinking, robbing a thief was not robbery at all!

For protection, the treasure ships would sail together in a large fleet which would be defended by enormous warships. One day Black Bart sailed his small fast ship into Bahai harbour, where forty Portuguese ships lay at anchor. So as to create a diversion in one corner of the harbour, he dragged two old ships behind him and set fire to them. While the warships were trying to put out the fire, Bart and his crew made off with the treasure ship *Sagrada Familia* and a twenty million pound fortune that was on its way to the King of Portugal!

Like any good Welshman Black Bart enjoyed literature and music. There was always a pipe band playing on his ship, and drummers from Africa. He used to sing a rousing war song before mounting an attack on a ship and, when he'd taken prisoners, he would entertain them in his cabin with cups of tea and a musical interlude while his thieves stole their cargo. He did not believe in using more violence than was necessary and any women passengers who fell into his hands were perfectly safe.

His one weakness was his love of colourful clothes. He was always finely dressed – he usually wore a red waistcoat, rich damask breeches, a hat with a red feather and, around his neck, a gold chain with a diamond cross. In his hand he would carry a shining sword and across his chest he wore a pair of pistols stuck in a red satin sash. He liked to swagger, loved wit and jokes, and as he was often seen in scarlet clothes, the French called him *'le joli rouge'*: 'the handsome one in red'.

Somehow *'Joli Rouge'* changed to *'Jolly Roger'* – and that became the name of the menacing pirate flag with the white skull and crossbones on a black background. It was Black Bart who designed the flag and he was the first to fly it on his ship. Whenever they saw that flag, the crews of the European merchant ships and warships knew they were about to fall prey to the famous Black Bart.

His name struck fear into Spanish, English and Portuguese sailors. He attacked their harbours and forts along the coast of West Africa, in the West Indies and in the Americas. In the space of two years he captured over four hundred ships and stole so much gold that he had to find a bigger ship for himself and two more ships to carry the treasure. The King of England offered him a pardon on condition that he gave up being a pirate – but Black Bart refused it.

For two and a half years every sailor was talking about him. To Europe's rulers he was a thorn in the side and they sent out fleets of ships to hunt him down, but Black Bart and his crew still managed to avoid them and to strike where they least expected.

Bart had acquired a ship called *The Royal*

Fortune. It was big and rather slow and awkward to manoeuvre. He didn't know it, but the English fleet was on his trail, and a man called Captain Ogle was out to get him.

On the 10th of February 1722 Black Bart was enjoying breakfast aboard *The Royal Fortune*, which was lying at anchor in a secluded bay at Parrot Island, off the coast of West Africa. Captain Ogle sailed up into view and he recognised the pirate flag.

A fierce and brutal battle followed. The pirate ship had been trapped and was a sitting target for the great guns of Captain Ogle's warship. When Black Bart came up on deck in his bright clothes to shout encouragement to his crew, he was an easy target and he was shot in the neck. The most successful pirate who ever lived fell and died on the deck of his ship.

So that was the end of Black Bart. But his legend did not die.

In fact the stories about his life, his personality and his extraordinary adventures grew and grew. As the golden age of pirates drew to a close, there was no doubt that Black Bart was the most famous of them all – he had stolen more treasure and captured more ships than any other pirate in history.

Stories about Bart reached Pembrokeshire. The inhabitants of the quiet inland village of Little Newcastle were secretly proud of the lad with the curly black hair who had sailed the seas and tormented the great rulers of the world with his pirate tricks. In time a large stone was erected on a strip of land in the middle of the village in memory of Black Bart, the famous pirate.

The poet I.D. Hooson wrote a lively ballad in Welsh that tells the story of Black Bart. Many children know these words by heart:

> 'Barti Ddu o Gasnewy' Bach,
> Y morwr tal a'r chwerthiniad iach,
>   Efô sydd y llyw
>   Ar y llong a'r criw:
> Barti Ddu o Gasnewy'Bach.'

Black Bart from Little Newcastle,
  The tall sailor with the merry laugh,
  He'll be at the helm
  Of his ship and his men:
Black Bart from Little Newcastle.